weight and weightlessness

Thomas Y. Crowell Company   New York

Weight AND Weightlessness

By Franklyn M. Branley · **Illustrated by Graham Booth**

LET'S-READ-AND-FIND-OUT SCIENCE BOOKS

Editors: *DR. ROMA GANS*, Professor Emeritus of Childhood Education, Teachers College, Columbia University

DR. FRANKLYN M. BRANLEY, Chairman and Astronomer of The American Museum–Hayden Planetarium

*AVAILABLE IN SPANISH

L.C. Card 70-132292   ISBN 0-690-87328-X   (Library Edition 0-690-87329-8)

How much do you weigh?
Suppose you weigh sixty pounds on the scale in your
bathroom. On a scale downtown, or at school, you
would also weigh sixty pounds. You would weigh
about sixty pounds on all scales here on earth.

If you were standing on a scale in a spaceship going around the earth, how much would you weigh? Not sixty pounds, not even ten pounds. You would weigh nothing at all. Your weight would be zero. You would be weightless.

Astronauts are weightless while they travel in space. They float around inside their spaceship unless they are fastened to their chairs or hold onto part of the spaceship.

Outside the ship, astronauts also float around in space. They must tie themselves to the spaceship so they will not float away.

When an astronaut lies on his couch inside the spaceship he does not feel the couch beneath him. He must fasten himself to the couch with straps. If he does not, he will float right out of bed.

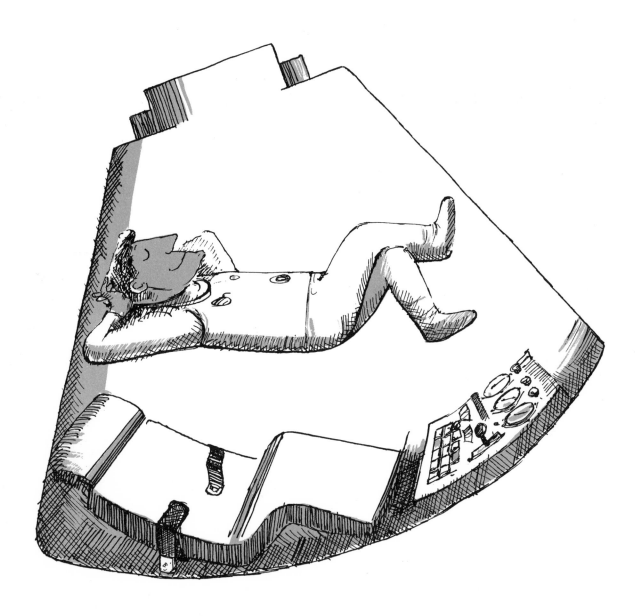

7

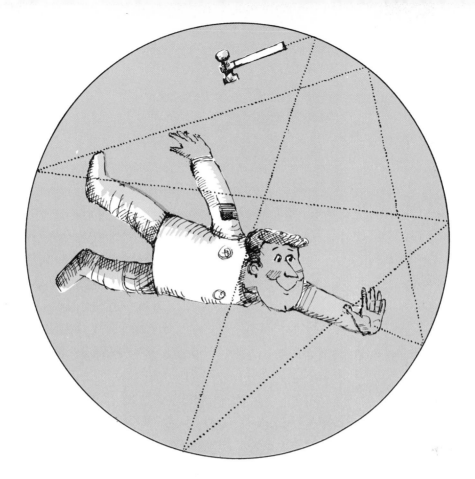

While a spaceship is going around the earth, everything inside it floats unless it is fastened down. If an astronaut lets go of a hammer, the hammer just stays there in the air. If he gives it a push, it will move until it hits something. Then it bounces and moves in another direction. That's because the hammer is weightless.

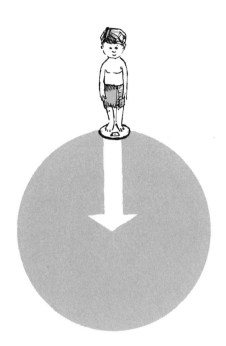

Let's find out why.

When you weigh yourself, you step on a scale. The gravity of the earth pulls you down onto the scale. Suppose you weigh sixty pounds. That means gravity is pulling you with a force of sixty pounds.

The scale tells how strongly gravity is pulling you down toward the center of the earth. If there were a deep hole under the scale, gravity would pull you all the way to the center of the earth.

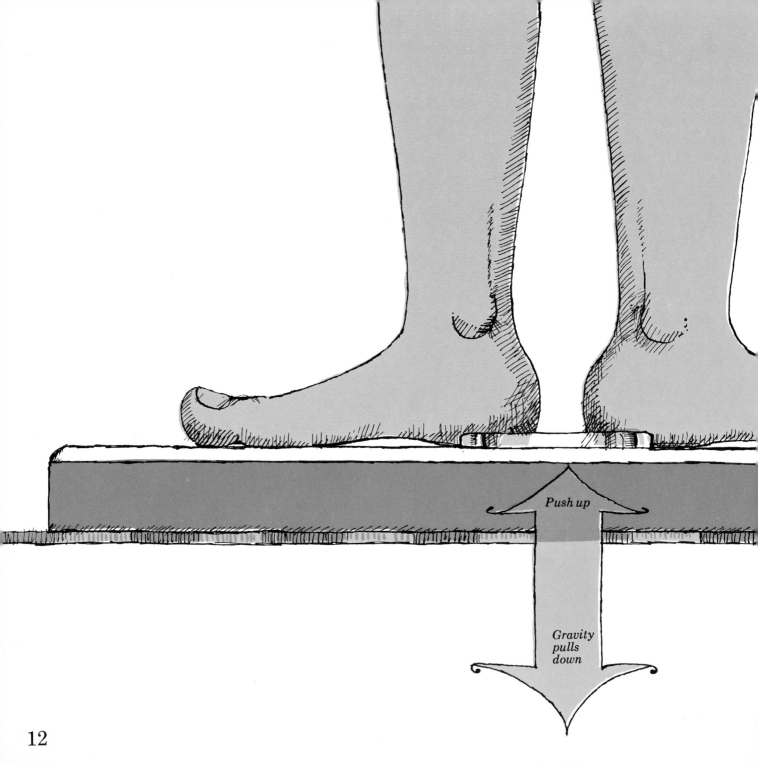

Push up

Gravity
pulls
down

But the scale and the floor beneath it keep you from being pulled to the center of the earth. They push up against gravity as gravity pulls down.

You can feel the pressure on the soles of your feet. That's what a scale really measures. It tells how much push upward there is against the pull of gravity downward.

Suppose, all of a sudden, there was a deep hole under the scale. And suppose you and the scale fell into the hole. You would not feel any push upward on the soles of your feet. There would be nothing pushing upward against the downward pull of gravity. Now the scale would read zero.

As long as you kept falling, you would be weightless.

That's why astronauts in spaceships are weightless. They are falling. Nothing is pushing back against them. They are falling around the earth. The astronauts are falling, the spaceship is falling, and so is everything inside it.

They do not look as if they were falling. But they are.

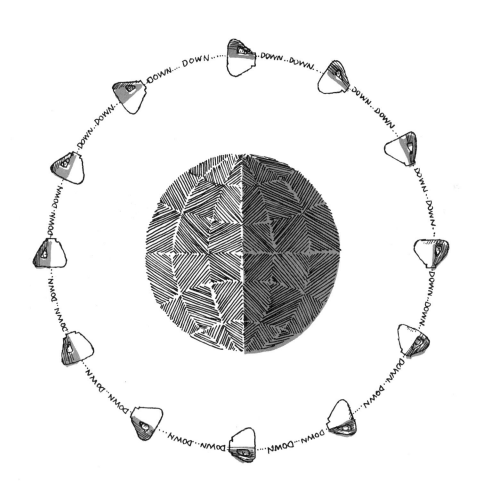

Here's the way it works.

Suppose a rocket was shot straight up from the
earth. The rocket would keep going up until its
fuel was gone. Then it would have no more power.

The rocket would coast upward. The earth's gravity would slow it down until it stopped. Then gravity would pull the rocket straight back to the earth.

17

If the rocket went up straight and then changed direction, gravity would still pull it back to the earth. But now the rocket would not come straight down. It would move in a curved path.

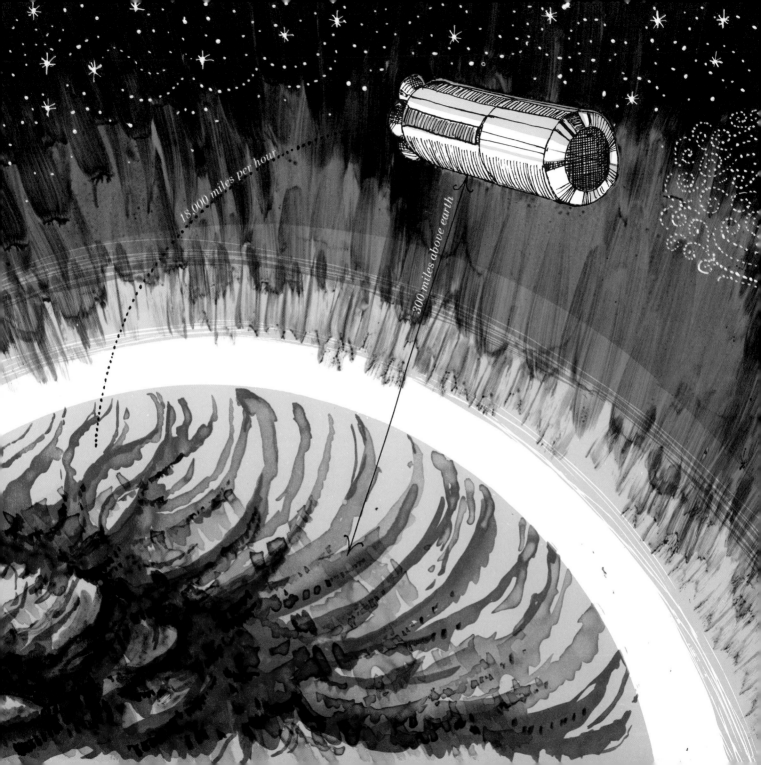

18,000 miles per hour

300 miles above earth

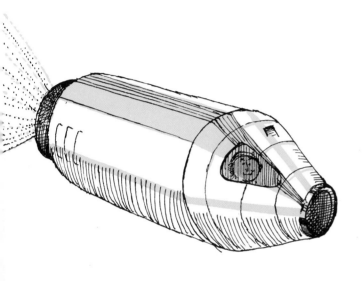

Let's say a rocket carries a spaceship 300 miles above the earth. The rocket and ship speed up to 18,000 miles an hour, then the ship separates from the rocket. Reverse jets slow down the rocket and gravity pulls it back down. The spaceship keeps going around the earth. It is really falling around the earth in a curved path.

But the ship doesn't get any closer to the earth.

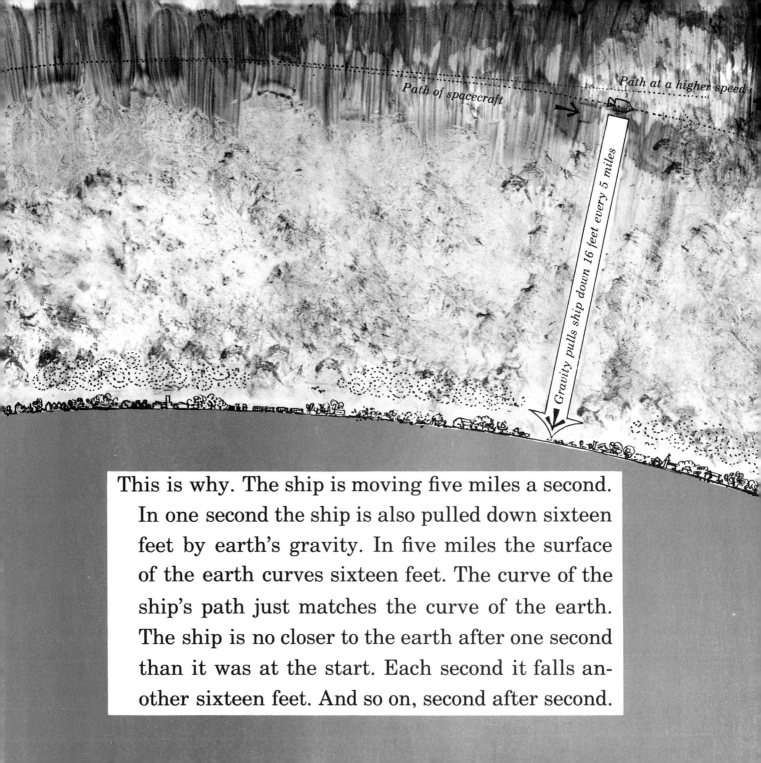

Path of spacecraft

Path at a higher speed

Gravity pulls ship down 16 feet every 5 miles

This is why. The ship is moving five miles a second. In one second the ship is also pulled down sixteen feet by earth's gravity. In five miles the surface of the earth curves sixteen feet. The curve of the ship's path just matches the curve of the earth. The ship is no closer to the earth after one second than it was at the start. Each second it falls another sixteen feet. And so on, second after second.

The ship is coasting around the earth. It is in orbit.
Everything is in orbit: the ship, the astronauts inside it, their food and drink, their tools and equip-
ment. Everything is in orbit, and everything is
weightless.

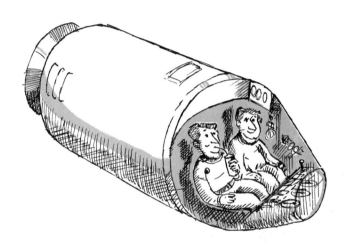

rotation for retrofire

retrofire

To make the ship return to the earth, the astronauts must change its path. First the ship must be slowed down. Retro-rockets do this. They act like brakes.

The curve of the ship's fall becomes steeper. Now it falls toward the earth more than sixteen feet each second. The curve of its path does not match the curve of the earth any longer. Gravity pulls the ship in closer and closer to the earth. The ship goes faster and faster toward the earth.

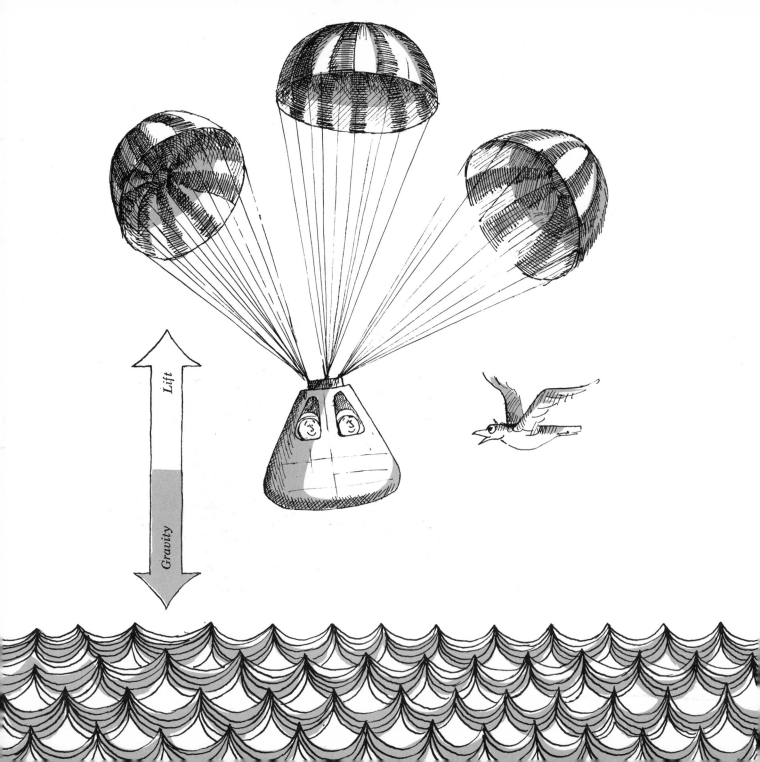

It has to be slowed down again or the ship will crash. Large parachutes aboard the spaceship are opened to fight the pull of gravity. Now the men feel the pull of gravity because the parachutes keep the ship from falling rapidly. If the men stood on a scale, they would now have weight.

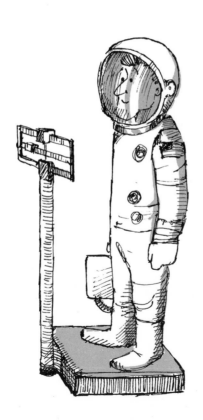

By the time the ship lands, the men weigh just as much as they did before. Once again something solid (the floor of the spaceship) pushes upward against the downward pull of gravity.

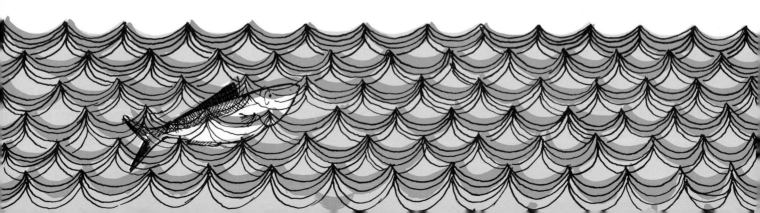

Astronauts like weightlessness for a while. It's fun to float in space. And it's funny to see things floating around you.

But after a while, an astronaut gets tired of being weightless. He likes to feel something solid under his feet when he stands up. And he likes to feel a bed under his back when he lies down. Also, it's nice to have food served on a plate, instead of squeezing it out of a tube.

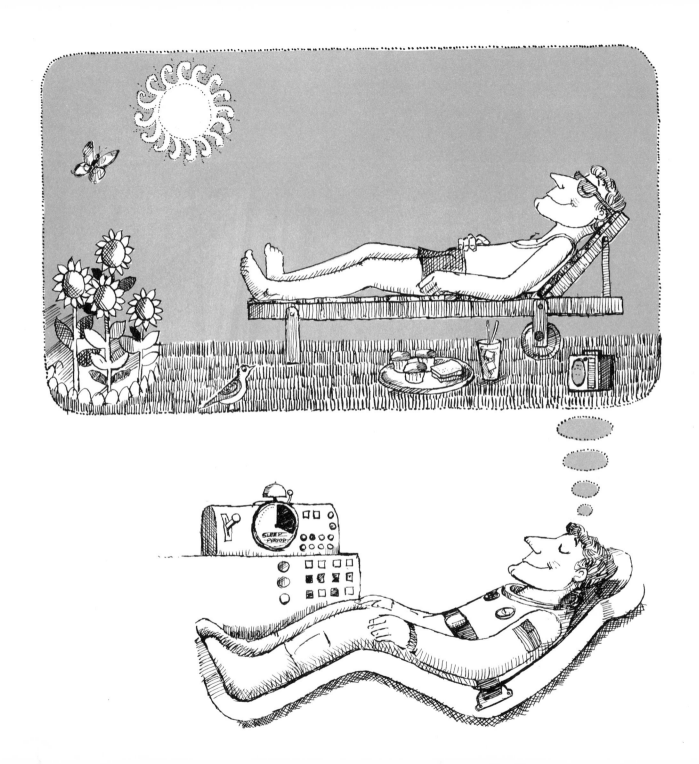

But I would like to try being weightless, for a while.
Wouldn't you?

ABOUT THE AUTHOR

Dr. Franklyn M. Branley is well known as the author of many excellent science books for young people of all ages. He is also co-editor of the Let's-Read-and-Find-Out Science Books.

Dr. Branley is Chairman and Astronomer of the American Museum-Hayden Planetarium in New York City. He is director of educational services for the Planetarium, where popular courses in astronomy, navigation, and meteorology are given for people of all ages. He is interested in all phases of astronomy and the national space program, and he instructs young people, adults, and teachers in these subjects.

Dr. Branley holds degrees from New York University, Columbia University, and from the New York State University College at New Paltz. He lives with his family in Woodcliff Lake, New Jersey.

ABOUT THE ARTIST

Graham Booth was born in London but grew up in Victoria, British Columbia. He was graduated from UCLA and received his master's degree in fine arts from the University of Southern California. Mr. Booth—author, designer, and active lecturer on the illustration of children's books—has appeared on numerous panels concerned with children's literature and has received many awards for his work. He presently teaches art at Fullerton Junior College.

Graham Booth lives in Laguna Beach, California, with his wife and two young sons. They summer on an island off the coast of British Columbia, where Mr. Booth paints and scuba dives for relaxation.

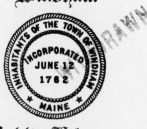